EXPLORING WATER

AND THE OCEAN

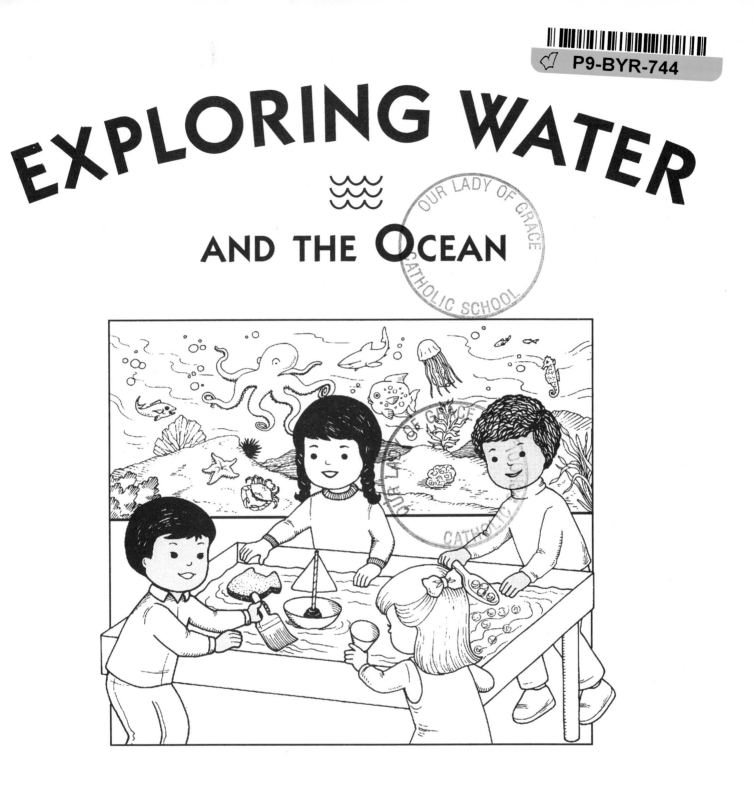

By Gayle Bittinger
Illustrations by Gary Mohrmann

TOTLINE® BOOKS

Warren Publishing House
Everett, WA

Some of the activity ideas in this book were originally contributed by *Totline Newsletter* subscribers. We wish to acknowledge:

Cathryn Abraham, St. Charles, IL; Lynn Beaird, Loma Linda, CA; Denise Bedell, Westland, MI; John M. Bittinger, Everett, WA; Janice Bodenstedt, Jackson, MI; Marjorie Debowy, Stony Brook, NY; Cindy Dingwall, Palatine, IL; Jan Dohman, West Point, IA; Barbara Dunn, Hollidaysburg, PA; Marion Ekberg, Gig Harbor, WA; Wes Epperson, Placerville, CA; Jeanne Feola, Verona, NY; Joan Giorgi, Massena, NY; Janet Helgaas, Luverne, MN; Ellen Javernick, Loveland, CO; Neoma Kreuter, Ontario, CA; Debra Lindahl, Libertyville, IL; Judith McNitt, Adrian, MI; Susan A. Miller, Kutztown, PA; Susan M. Paprocki, Northbrook, IL; Susan Peters, Upland, CA; Sue Schliecker, Waukesha, WI; Diane Thom, Maple Valley, WA; Cheryl B. Vlach, Stanwood, WA; Nancy Windes, Denver, CO; Jean Woods, Tulsa, OK.

Editorial Staff:
    Editorial Manager: Kathleen Cubley
    Contributing Editors: Elizabeth McKinnon, Jean Warren
    Copy Editor: Brenda Mann Harrison
    Editorial Assisant: Erica West

Design and Production Staff:
    Art Manager: Jill Lustig
    Book Design/Layout: Sarah Ness
    Cover: Eric Stovall
    Production Manager: JoAnna Brock

ISBN 0-911019-59-6

Library of Congress Catalog Number 92-62462
Printed in the United States of America
Published by: Warren Publishing House
              P.O. Box 2250
              Everett, WA 98203

20 19 18 17 16 15 14 13 12 11 10 9 8 7 6 5 4

INTRODUCTION

~~~

When children have opportunities to manipulate water, they learn about basic math and science concepts, use language to describe what is happening and develop fine and gross motor skills.

Exploring Water takes advantage of children's natural interest in water and provides stepping stones to other opportunities for learning. After the chapter of beginning water table activities, there is a chapter filled with ideas for using water around the curriculum. From water in the art area to water music, there are a variety of activities to help children explore water in new ways.

Learning occurs more readily for young children when they can move from the known to the unknown, and this book is arranged with that in mind. As your children become more familiar with water, you can expand their interest into the ocean. Place two or three plastic whales in the water table. Tell your children that whales are found in the ocean. As your children's curiosity is piqued, use the activities in the ocean portion of the book to expand on it. Each topic of the ocean is followed by quick facts for your information, to share with your children as you feel appropriate.

As with all Totline books, *Exploring Water* is designed to be an easy-to-use reference tool, not a planned curriculum guide. You are encourage to use whichever activities fit the needs and interests of your children. All of the activities in this book are appropriate for young children and use materials that are readily available.

With *Exploring Water* as a resource, you and your children will enjoy the journey from water to ocean and back again.

CONTENTS

≋

Exploring Water

Exploring the Ocean

Ocean Preservation

Ocean Patterns

Children's Book List 90

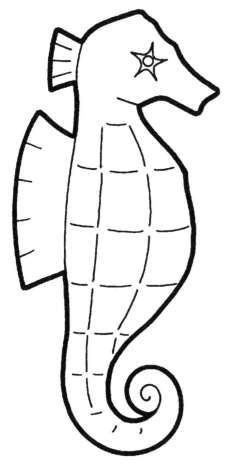

Water Table Fun

Basic Water Table Props

Set out a variety of the items listed below for your children to play and experiment with at the water table.

- balloons filled with water
- basters
- blown-up balloons
- bowls
- clear-plastic containers
- dish mops
- dishpans
- eyedroppers
- funnels
- margarine tubs
- measuring cups
- measuring spoons
- paintbrushes
- Ping-Pong balls
- pitchers
- scoops
- sieves
- sponges
- spoons
- spray bottles
- straws
- rotary eggbeaters
- whisks

Shower Bottles

Cut the bottoms off baby-powder containers and fill them with water. Let your children open and close the tops of the containers to make showers in the water table.

Sprinklers

Clean and rinse empty soup cans. Punch holes around each can about 1 inch up from the bottom. Have your children fill the cans with water and watch it sprinkle out.

Sponge Bucket

Place a variety of colors and sizes of sponges in a bucket for your children to play with at the water table. To make the sponges more fun to play with, cut them into the shapes of animals, people, boats, flowers, etc.

Water Table Fun

9

Soap Bars

Place a variety of sizes and colors of soap bars, including some regular bars of soap and some Ivory soap bars, in the water table. Let your children discover which soap bars float and which ones sink. (The Ivory soap bars float because they are less dense than water; the regular soap bars sink because they are more dense.) Then let your children use the bars to lather up, wash their hands, and make bubbles in the water.

Cruise Liner

Cut the bottom half off a plastic-foam egg carton and float it in the water table to make a "cruise liner." Collect 12 Ping-Pong balls, corks or bottle caps for "passengers." Use a permanent felt-tip marker to add faces to the balls, corks or caps. Let your children take turns putting the passengers in the egg-cup "cabins" of the cruise liner.

Marbles

Collect marbles of various sizes and colors. Place the marbles on the bottom of the water table. Add other water table props as desired. Let your children play with the marbles in the table.

Clear-Plastic Bottle

Cut in half an empty 2-liter clear-plastic soft-drink bottle. Remove the opaque base, if there is one, from the bottom half. Have your children use the top half as a funnel by taking off the cap and turning it upside down. Let them use the bottom half as an underwater viewer by pressing it partway into the water and looking through it at items in the water table.

Water Table Fun

Sinkers and Floaters

Put items that sink (such as marbles, metal toy cars, rocks and silverware) and items that float (such as corks, pieces of wood, plastic boats and sponges) in a box. Let your children experiment with the items in the water table to discover which ones sink and which ones float.

Variation: Collect a variety of fruits and vegetables. Let your children discover which ones float and which ones sink.

Make It Float

Let your children experiment with shapes that float and shapes that sink. Set out balls of clay. What happens when they put a ball of clay in the water? (It sinks.) Ask your children to try to shape the clay so that it will float. (Boat shapes float.)

Boat Making

Set out milk cartons, walnut halves, plastic-foam trays, wood scraps, and other containers that float to use as ship hulls. Set out waxed paper, construction paper, fabric scraps and pieces of vinyl, plus straws and craft sticks to make sails. In addition, provide glue, scissors and crayons. Let your children use these materials to make their own boats. When all the boats are completed, let your children float their creations in the water table.

Balancing-Act Barges

Place plastic-foam food trays in the water table. Have your children place small objects onto each food-tray "barge" so that a "balancing act," not a sinking act, occurs.

Water Table Fun

Egg-Boat Floating

Cut all of the egg cups out of a plastic-foam egg carton. Gather small items such as pennies, small toys, cotton balls and golf balls. Put the egg cups in the water table. Let your children add the items to the cups. How many pennies can be added to one cup before it sinks or tips over? Can the same number of cotton balls be added to another cup? Have your children try floating each object in the egg-boat floaters.

Arctic Ice Play

Fill the water table with comfortably warm water. Add several trays of ice cubes, one tray at a time, to the water. Ask your children to observe what happens to the water temperature and the ice cubes. Ask them to explain the difference between the temperature of the water and the temperature of the ice cubes. Then let your children float toy boats through the ice-cube "icebergs."

Estimating

Put 1-cup measuring cups and large plastic containers in the water table. Show your children one of the containers. Ask them to guess how many cups of water will fit into that container. Then pour cups of water into the container, one at a time, and have the children count with you.

Siphon Fun

Cut plastic tubing into various lengths. Place the tubing in the water table. Let your children experiment with the tubing and discover how water moves through it. Then show your children how to siphon water from the water table to a bucket on the floor. Select a length of tubing that reaches from the table to the bucket. Fill the tubing with water and cover both ends with your thumbs. Place one end in the water table and take your thumb off it. Put the other end in the bucket, remove your thumb and let your children watch water move from the water table to the bucket.

Water Ball

Fill two empty 2-liter soft-drink bottles with water (or use two un-opened bottles). Place them at one end of the water table. Tie a length of string or yarn to the tops of the bottles to resemble a goal line. Let your children blow through straws to propel a plastic-foam ball or Ping-Pong ball under the goal line.

Water Alternatives

Besides water, let your children explore and experiment with the following alternatives.

Snow — Fill the water table with snow. Have your children wear mittens while playing in it.

Warm Water — Put warm water in the water table and let your children play in it. Add more warm water as necessary to keep the desired temperature.

Bubbles — Add liquid dishwashing detergent to the water in the water table. Show your children how to stir up bubbles with a rotary eggbeater, a whisk or their hands.

Colored Water — Add a few drops of food coloring to the water in the water table to make colorful water for your children to play with.

Gelatin — Make several large batches of gelatin (plain or flavored). Cut the gelatin into squares and place them in the water table for your children to explore with their hands. Or make gelatin in dishpans for your children to play with.

Individual Water Tables

Prepare any of the following water tables for your children to play in one at a time.

Dishpan — Fill a dishpan with water and place it on a towel on a low table.

Plastic Tub for Infants — Place a plastic bathtub for infants on the floor or a chair and fill it partway with water.

Sink — Fill a sink with water and set a stool in front of it. Let a child stand on the stool and play in the water.

Large Water Tables

Prepare any of the following water tables for water play by two or three children at a time.

Bathtub — Fill a bathtub with water. Let two or three of your children kneel at the edge of the bathtub to play in the water.

Laundry Tub — Cut the legs off an old laundry tub so that the tub is the desired height. Stand the tub on the floor. Plug the hole with a stopper and fill the tub with water.

Wading Pool — Set up an inflatable or plastic wading pool and fill it partway with water.

Learning With Water

Water Painting

Set out paintbrushes, pieces of dark construction paper and shallow containers filled with water. Let your children dip the brushes into the water and then "paint" pictures on the construction paper. Encourage them to observe the changes in their pictures as the water soaks in, evaporates, and then disappears.

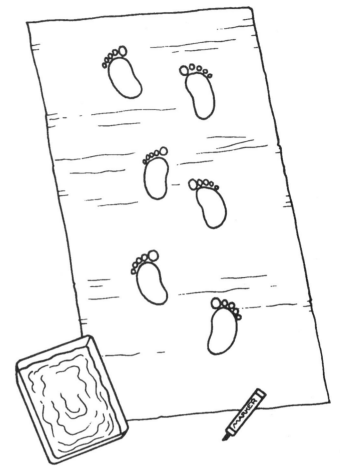

Water Footprints

Cut large paper bags apart at the seams and lay them flat on the floor. Set out two or three pans of water. Have your children take off their shoes and socks. Let them take turns stepping into the pans of water and walking across the paper bags to leave their footprints. Outline some of the footprints with a permanent marker. As the water evaporates and the footprints disappear, let the children make more footprints.

Variation: Let your children make hand prints instead of footprints.

Splatter Paintings

Have your children paint designs on construction paper with different colors of tempera paint. While the paintings are still wet, take them outside and lay them flat on the sidewalk. Let the children splatter water on their paintings with spray bottles. Have the children watch as the colors on their paintings run and mix together.

Colored-Water Designs

Fill the cups of several muffin tins with water. Add food coloring to the cups, making as many different colors as desired. Set out the muffin tins, eyedroppers and paper towels. Show your children how to squeeze the eyedroppers so they fill with colored water. Then have them drip-drop the water on the paper towels to make designs.

Paint Washes

Have your children use crayons to draw pictures on construction paper. (Have them press down hard with the crayons to make solid lines.) Make a paint wash by diluting tempera paint with water. Then let the children brush the paint wash over their papers with paintbrushes to make the crayon drawings stand out.

Bubble Art

Fill several large containers partway with water and add food coloring as desired. Then add enough liquid dishwashing detergent to each container to make colored bubble soap. Give each of your children a bubble-blowing wand. Let them dip their wands in the colored bubble mixtures and blow bubbles onto white tissue paper. Allow the tissue paper to dry. If desired, let the children use their Bubble-Art as wrapping paper.

Variation: Have your children blow colorful bubbles on paper towels. After the paper towels dry, use them as napkins at snacktime.

Spray Painting

Fill several spray bottles with thinned tempera paint. Hang pieces of paper inside or outdoors on a wall, an easel or a clothesline. Let your children use the bottles to spray-paint pictures on the papers.

Watercolor Painting

Make watercolor paint for your children by pouring various colors of leftover tempera paint into the egg cups of egg cartons. Allow the paint to dry. Cut each egg carton into 4-cup sections. Give each of your children one of the sections, a paintbrush, a cup of water and a piece of paper. Show them how to dip their brushes in water and then on the dried paint to make watercolors.

Learning With Water

Examining Water

Collect a variety of water types such as distilled, tap, puddle, lake, ocean and bath. Place each type in a clear-plastic cup and label it. Set out the cups and a magnifying glass. Let your children take turns using the magnifying glass to examine the different kinds of water. Ask them to describe what they see in the water in each cup.

Water Wheel

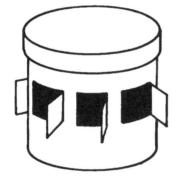

Cut a cylindrical oatmeal box in half. Remove the lid and put it on the top of the bottom half of the box. Discard the top half. Cut six flaps around the middle of the cylinder and bend them back as shown in the illustration. Poke a hole through the top and bottom of the box, and push a dowel or an unsharpened pencil through them. Turn on a faucet. Hold onto the dowel with both hands and position the flaps on the cylinder under the running water so that the water wheel spins.

What Dissolves?

Have your children watch as you stir a spoonful of sugar into a glass of water. Where did the sugar go? Explain to the children that the water separated the sugar into tiny pieces, called molecules, that cannot be seen. The water *dissolved* the sugar. Set out glasses of water, spoons and small bowls of sugar, salt, flour, rice and other kitchen items as desired. Let your children experiment with them. Which items dissolve in water? Which ones do not?

Water in the Air

Ask your children to tell you where they can find water. Tell them that water is also found in the air. Then show them this experiment. Place an empty glass on a table and fill it with ice cubes. After 5 to 10 minutes, drops of water will form on the outside of the glass. Tell your children that the water on the outside of the glass came from the air. This is called *condensation*. Condensation happens when water particles in the air become cold enough to change into drops of water.

Learning With Water

Capillary Action

Set out a small plate and a bowl of water with lots of food coloring added to it. Place one end of a strip of cotton fabric in the bowl and the other end on the small plate. Ask your children to guess what will happen. In 5 to 10 minutes, the water will travel from the bowl, across the fabric and onto the plate. Explain to the children that the water is moving because of *capillary action*. Capillary action is the tendency of water to move through tiny hair-width passageways, like those found in fabric. Capillary action is also how water moves from a tree's roots to its outermost branches.

Moving Water

Fill an eyedropper with colored water. Place the eyedropper in a glass of clear water. Have the children watch as the colored water from the eyedropper moves into the clear water. Water is made up of tiny molecules that are constantly moving. The molecules are invisible to the naked eye, but their motion can be seen by the moving of the colored water through the clear water.

Learning With Water

Water Books

Cut out magazine pictures of water (water in nature, water in bottles and glasses, people using water, etc.). Give each of your children several pieces of construction paper. Have the children select pictures and glue them to their papers. Allow the glue to dry, then add a cover and staple each child's book together. Write "Water Book by *Child's Name*" on the each cover. Let your children take turns "reading" their water books to you and to one another.

Listening Game

Fill four glasses with different levels of water. Carefully strike each glass with a spoon. Each glass will make a different sound. Challenge your children to listen for the differences. Which glass makes the highest sound? Which glass makes the lowest sound? When water is added or removed from a glass, how does the sound change?

Learning With Water

Water Fingerplay

As you read the following rhyme to your children, have them point to the appropriate body parts as they are mentioned.

Water, water everywhere,

On my face and on my hair,

On my fingers, on my toes,

Water, water on my nose!

Jean Warren

Water Story

Collect a variety of items that can be associated with water such as a cup, a straw, a package of instant soup, a pitcher, a sponge and a bar of soap. Put the items into a bag. Have your children sit in a circle. Pull out one of the items and begin to tell a story about water that mentions the selected item. Then pause and let a child draw another item out of the bag. Weave that item into the plot of your water story. Continue until each child has had a turn or until all the water items have been drawn out of the bag.

Variation: Let older children draw items out of the bag and continue the story themselves.

Empty to Full

Collect five empty clear-plastic soft drink bottles of the same size. Put a different amount of water in each bottle, leaving one bottle empty and filling one bottle completely. Screw the lids tightly on the bottles. Let your children take turns lining up the bottles from empty to full.

Pouring Water

Show your children clear-plastic cups that are filled with varying amounts of water. Talk about which cup has the most water or the least water and which one is full or half-full, etc. Then give each of your children a clear-plastic cup and a small pitcher of water with a few drops of food coloring added to it. Let the children pour varying amounts of water into their cups. Then have them pour the water back into the pitchers. Let them continue pouring the water back and forth as long as interest lasts.

Learning With Water

29

Ice Cube Estimation

Select three or four clear containers of various shapes and sizes, such as a cup, a bowl, a pitcher and a vase. Show your children an ice cube. Ask them to estimate how many ice cubes will fit in each container. Count the ice cubes as you place them into the containers. Were the children's guesses too high, too low or just right? Then ask the children to estimate how high the water from the melted ice cubes will be in each container. Mark their guesses with strips of masking tape. After the ice cubes melt, have the children compare the actual level of the water with their guesses.

Counting Drops

Set out five small bowls numbered from 1 to 5. Give one of your children a glass of water and an eyedropper. Have the child use the eyedropper to put the appropriate number of water drops in each bowl.

More or Less

Collect several 8-ounce containers such as a baby bottle, a short glass, a tall glass, a bowl, etc. It is important that all the containers hold *exactly* 8 ounces. Show your children a measuring cup that has ounce markings on the sides. Show them where the mark for 8 ounces is and underline it with colored tape. Fill the measuring cup with water to the 8-ounce marking. Ask the children which container they think the water will fit in. Pour the water into that container. Ask the children if they think the water will fit in any other container. Then let the children watch as you pour 8 ounces of water into each of the other containers. This is an excellent way to introduce the concept of volume. Explain that objects can have different shapes but still have the same volume, which means they can hold the same amount of water.

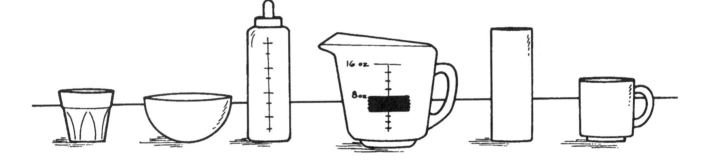

What Is Missing?

Fill a plastic dishpan with water. Float several objects on top of the water. Show the dishpan and floating objects to your children. Ask them to cover their eyes while you remove one of the objects. Then have the children open their eyes and guess which object was removed. Let the child who guesses correctly remove the object the next time.

Splash Dance

Collect two swimming masks and two pairs of fins. Fill a wading pool with water. Have your children wear bathing suits. Select two children to put on the masks and fins and step into the pool. Play some music and have the children in the pool splash and dance around. Repeat until each child has had a turn.

Funnel Game

Divide your children into two teams. Place two buckets of water on one side of an outdoor area and two empty buckets on the other side. Have each team stand by one of the buckets of water. Give the first child in each team a funnel. When you say, "Go," have the children with the funnels fill them with water, hold their fingers under the spouts, carefully walk to the empty buckets and let the water drain out of their funnels and into the buckets. Then have them hurry back and give their funnels to the next children in line. Continue until each child has had a turn or until a designated time is up.

Water Song

Sung to: "The Wheels on the Bus"

Water is wet and it pours like this,

Pours like this, pours like this.

Water is wet and it pours like this,

See how it goes.

Let your children pour water while singing this song.

Gayle Bittinger

The Water Goes Drip-Drop

Sung to: "The Farmer in the Dell"

The water goes drip-drop,

The water goes drip-drop.

Drip-drop, how it does plop,

The water goes drip-drop.

The water goes splish-splash,

The water goes splish-splash.

Splish-splash, how it does dash,

The water goes splish-splash.

Gayle Bittinger

Learning With Water

We're So Lucky

Sung to: "Mary Had a Little Lamb"

We're so lucky to have water,

To have water, to have water.

We're so lucky to have water,

We can take our baths in it.

Repeat, letting your children name other things they can do with water.

Jean Woods

See the Water

Sung to: "Frere Jacques"

See the water, see the water,

Every day, every day.

Water is a helper,

Water is a helper.

I know how, I know how.

See the water, see the water,

Every day, every day.

We wash clothes in water,

(Pretend to wash clothes in water.)

We wash clothes in water.

I know how, I know how.

See the water, see the water,

Every day, every day.

We sprinkle plants with water,

(Pretend to water plants.)

We sprinkle plants with water.

I know how, I know how.

Continue with additional verses as desired.

Cheryl B. Vlach

Learning With Water

Water Snacks

Take advantage of snacktime to demonstrate and discuss what happens when water is boiled, frozen, evaporated and used to dilute. For example, you can boil water to make noodles or hard-cooked eggs; freeze water to make frozen pops or ice cubes with fruit pieces inside; dry fruits to demonstrate evaporation; dilute juice concentrate with water to make fruit juice.

Snow Cones

To make each cone, place crushed ice in a paper cup. Mix one part unsweetened frozen apple-juice or orange-juice concentrate with one part water. Pour the diluted concentrate over the ice.

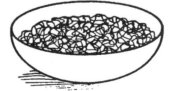

Learning With Water

In the Ocean

Ocean Facts

■ All the waters of the oceans comprise 97 percent of the earth's water. They also cover 70 percent of the earth's surface and form one connected body of water, called the world ocean. (This can be easily seen on a globe.)

■ The world ocean is made up of four major oceans. These oceans are, in order of size, the Pacific Ocean, the Atlantic Ocean, the Indian Ocean and the Artic Ocean. The remaining seas, gulfs and bays are considered parts of these four oceans.

■ The ocean floor has enormous mountains and valleys, much taller and deeper than those on land. When the mountains rise above the ocean's surface, they form islands.

■ The depth of the ocean varies from just a few inches along a beach to more than 6 miles down into a valley in the middle of the ocean. The average depth of the ocean is 12,200 feet.

■ Oceans are filled with animal and plant life. These animals and plants are an important source of food for humans.

Sculpting the Ocean

Explain to your children that the bottom, or floor, of the ocean is not flat; it has hills, mountains and valleys just as those found on land. Then divide your children into small groups. Give each group a clear-glass baking pan and some clay. Have the groups use the clay to form ocean floors in the bottoms of their pans. As the groups finish, let them pour water over their ocean floors. Have them look at their oceans from all sides. Are any parts of their ocean floors sticking above the water? Those are islands.

Cross the Ocean Game

Cut small and large island shapes out of construction paper. Tape the shapes to the floor. Tell your children that the floor is the ocean. Ask them to cross the ocean by stepping only on the island shapes.

In the Ocean

Sung to: "Mary Had a Little Lamb"

In the ocean you will find,

You will find, you will find,

In the ocean you will find,

Many kinds of fish.

Repeat, substituting the names of other things that might be found in the ocean for *Many kinds of fish.*

Gayle Bittinger

In the Ocean

Ocean Beach Facts

■ Ocean beaches are sandy, rocky or muddy edges of land along the edge of the ocean.

■ Many plants and animals live on the ocean beach.

■ Shells, rocks, logs and other "treasures" can be found on the beach, because powerful ocean waves carry things from other places.

■ At different times throughout a day, ocean beaches can be dry or covered with water as the ocean tides go in and out.

Ocean Beach Art

Set out pieces of light-blue posterboard, paintbrushes, glue and a box of sand. Let your children make "beaches" on the pieces of posterboard by brushing glue across the bottoms of them and sprinkling on sand. Have them shake off any excess sand into the box. Then give your children small shells, shell pieces and rocks to glue on their beach scenes. If desired, give each child a yellow construction-paper sun shape to glue at the top of his or her paper.

In the Ocean

Beach Story

Let your children take turns filling in the blanks in the following open-ended story about the beach.

I went to the beach today.

The sun was as hot as _____.

The sky was as blue as _____.

The ocean was as cold as _____.

I swam in the water just like a _____.

I played in the sand and built a _____.

While I was walking around, I found a _____.

I love to run on the beach like a _____.

I had fun at the beach.

Jean Warren

Walking on the Beach

Sung to: "The Farmer in the Dell"

Walking on the beach,

Walking on the beach,

When you're walking on the beach,

You might find a shell.

Repeat, substituting the names of other things that might be found on a beach for *shell*.

Gayle Bittinger

In the Ocean

Sea Water Facts

■ Sea water tastes and smells salty. Although sea water is saltier in some parts of the ocean than others, most sea water averages 3.5 percent salt. The salt in sea water is mostly table salt.

■ Sea water also contains all the minerals found on land.

■ When sea water evaporates, the salt and other minerals are left behind.

■ Objects float more easily in salty sea water than in plain water because sea water is more dense and can support more weight.

Collecting Sea Salt

If you live near the ocean, collect some sea water as far away from sewers or drainage as possible and as far out as possible. (Or, if you don't live near the ocean, make your own sea water by purchasing synthetic sea salt from a fish store and mixing the water and salts as directed.) Show your children the sea water. Let them smell the water. Then let them watch as you put some of the sea water in a pan and heat it to evaporate the water. When the water has evaporated, salt will remain.

Sea Salt Art

Mix liquid tempera paint with a small amount of salt. Give each of your children a spoon and a piece of finger-paint paper or a brown paper bag. Put a spoonful of paint on each child's paper. Let the children push their paint around with their spoons. Add more paint or salt as needed.

The Sea Is Salty

Sung to: "Mary Had a Little Lamb"

The water in the sea is salty,

Sea is salty, sea is salty,

The water in the sea is salty,

As salty as can be.

When sea water dries all up,

Dries all up, dries all up,

When sea water dries all up,

A pile of salt you'll see.

Gayle Bittinger

Ocean Wave Facts

■ Wind causes most ocean waves. Waves are always moving.

■ The water in a wave moves up and down, not forward. Only water in a wave that hits land moves forward (such as the water in a wave breaking onto a beach).

■ Waves that keep hitting a certain part of the earth can cut away sloping land and make cliffs. They can also break up rocks to form beaches.

■ A special kind of ocean wave is set off by an earthquake on the sea floor. This wave is called a *tsunami* (sue-nah-mee). Tsunamis can travel as fast as 600 miles per hour on the open sea. Eventually they slow down, build in height and may crash onto land. Tsunamis occur mostly in the Pacific Ocean.

Making Waves

Fill a small plastic jar two-thirds full with water. Add a couple drops blue food coloring and mix well. Fill the rest of the jar with mineral oil, getting rid of as many air bubbles as possible. Secure the lid. Let your children hold the bottle sideways and gently tip it to create waves.

Extension: Let your children make waves by shaking a rope that has one end tied to a chair. Encourage them to observe how the waves make the rope move up and down, while the rope does not move forward. This is like the waves in the ocean — the waves move forward, but the water just moves up and down.

In the Ocean

Moving Objects

Float a toy in one end of a water table, pool or bathtub. Ask your children to move the toy to the other end of the water table by making waves. Explain to your children that this is the same way that logs and debris are moved by waves across the ocean.

The Waves Are Moving

Sung to: "When Johnny Comes Marching Home"

The waves are moving across the sea,

   hurrah, hurrah,

The waves are moving across the sea,

   hurrah, hurrah.

The waves are moving constantly,

They move so fast across the sea.

Oh, the waves are moving so fast

   across the sea.

Gayle Bittinger

Tide Pool Facts

■ Tide pools are created when water brought in with the tide fills the dips and crevasses in the sand and rocks on the beach.

■ Tide pools are covered with water when the tide is in and exposed when the tide is out. Most tide pools have at least some water in them all the time.

■ Tide pools are homes to many different kinds of animals (such as sea stars, sculpins and anemone) and plants (such as seaweed). The animals and plants of a tide pool live because of the fresh sea water and food brought in by each high tide.

How Many in the Pool?

Cut five tide pool shapes out of felt. Number the shapes from 1 to 5. Cut shapes of tide pool animals and plants (such as sea stars, sculpins, anemones and seaweed) out of felt, so that there are 15 shapes total. Place the tide pools on a flannelboard. Have your children take turns arranging the animal and plant shapes on the tide pools so that there are the appropriate number of shapes on each pool.

In the Ocean

In and Out

Explain to your children that when the tide comes in, the animals in the tide pools are busy eating and collecting food. When the tide goes out, the animals keep still to conserve energy. Have your children pretend to be animals in a tide pool. When you say "In," have your children move around, pretending to collect and eat food. When you say "Out," have them lie still.

What's in It?

Sung to: "Skip to My Lou"

See the tide pool, what's in it?

See the tide pool, what's in it?

See the tide pool, what's in it?

What's in it today?

I see a sculpin in the tide pool,

I see a sculpin in the tide pool,

I see a sculpin in the tide pool,

In the tide pool today.

Repeat, substituting *sculpin* with the names of other things you might find in a tide pool.

Gayle Bittinger

In the Ocean

Seaweed Facts

■ Any plant that grows in the sea can be called seaweed; however, botaninsts (plant experts) refer to seaweed as only brown, red and green algae.

■ Seaweed grows along the coastlines of most parts of the world ocean, from polar seas to tropical waters. Seaweed "beds," the places where a lot of seaweed grows in one spot, provide food and protection for many animals.

■ Most seaweed is edible and can be eaten raw or cooked.

■ Various kinds of seaweed are found in many products, from medicines and make-up to soft drinks and condiments. For example, sea lettuce is used in soups and salads and brewed in tea. Carageenan, made from several kinds of seaweed, is used as a thickening agent in many kinds of hand lotion, cough syrup, chocolate milk, toothpaste, ice cream and cottage cheese.

Seaweed Mural

Cut out magazine pictures of seaweed and pictures of foods and products that might have seaweed in them (dairy products, soft drinks, soups, salads, make-up, spices, etc.) Set out a long piece of butcher paper. Let your children glue the pictures to the paper to create a Seaweed Mural.

Seaweed Gelatin

Purchase *Agar Agar* flakes (also known as *Kanten*) from a natural foods store. Show the Agar Agar flakes to your children and explain that the flakes are seaweed that has been boiled, pressed into a thick gel, and dried. Then make gelatin with the Agar Agar. Put 4 cups of any kind of juice (except orange juice) in a saucepan. Sprinkle 2 tablespoons Agar Agar flakes over the top of the juice. Bring the juice to a boil, reduce heat, and simmer 5 minutes or until the flakes are dissolved. Chill until firm. If desired, add cut-up fruits and vegetables to the gelatin before chilling it.

Seaweed Grows

Sung to: "Three Blind Mice"

Seaweed grows, seaweed grows,

In the sea, in the sea.

Seaweed grows in brown, red and green,

It's the prettiest algae you've ever seen,

If you find some, then you'll know what I mean.

Seaweed grows.

Gayle Bittinger

In the Ocean

Scuba Diver Facts

■ The word scuba originated as an acronym for self-contained under-water breathing apparatus.

■ The first scuba gear was the Aqualung. It was invented in 1943 by Jacques-Yves Cousteau and Emil Gagnan of France.

■ Scuba diving, unlike deep-sea diving, requires no air lines or hoses from the diver to the surface. It is often called free diving.

■ A scuba diver wears a tank of pressurized air. A mouthpiece helps regulate the air as it is breathed in and out.

■ Scuba divers can dive up to 130 feet below sea level.

Diver Dress-Up

Collect a variety of diving equipment such as masks, fins, snorkels, wet suits, etc. Let your children look at and try on the equipment.

Variation: Make diver's masks and oxygen tanks as described below. Set out the masks and tanks and let your children put them on.

Diver's Masks — Cut 2½-inch sections out of cylindrical oatmeal boxes. In each section, cut a notch in one end (to fit over a child's nose) and cover the other end with a piece of clear plastic wrap secured with a rubber band. Cover the outsides of the sections with construction paper. Attach thick yarn ties to the sides of the masks.

Oxygen Tanks — Rinse and dry bleach bottles. Attach two ribbons to the top and bottom of each bottle as shown in the illustration. If desired, use a permanent marker to write "Oxygen" on each bottle. Have your children slip their arms through the ribbons to wear the tanks on their backs.

Movement Fun

Invite your children to join you for some fun in the ocean. Pass out imaginary scuba masks and have the children pretend to put them on and dive under the water. What do they see? Have the children name different things they might see underwater in the ocean, such as fish, seaweed, sharks, whales and octopuses.

I Love to Dive
Sung to: "My Bonnie Lies Over the Ocean"

I love to dive in the ocean,

I love to dive in the sea,

I love to dive in water,

Oh, won't you come dive with me?

Dive, dive, dive, dive,

Oh, won't you come dive with me?

Dive, dive, dive, dive,

Oh, come dive in the ocean with me.

Jean Warren

In the Ocean

Ocean Animals

Coral Facts

■ Coral animals are generally found in warm and tropical seas. They have cylindrical bodies that are usually less than 1 inch in diameter. Coral animals can be a variety of colors such as tan, orange, yellow, purple and green.

■ Each coral animal has one end that attaches itself to a hard surface and one end that has a mouth with tiny tentacles. The coral uses its tentacles to eat algae that floats by.

■ Over time coral animals produce calcium carbonate (limestone) that collects around the lower halves of their bodies. As a group of coral animals grow, the limestone deposits become bigger and bigger. When coral grows in a line horizontal or perpendicular to the coastline, the deposits are called a reef. When coral grows on a sunken bank or the crater of a volcano that has sunk below the surface of the sea, it is called an atoll.

■ The largest construction on earth, bigger than any man-made structure, is the Great Barrier Reef off the coast of Australia.

Coral Building

Have your children pretend they are coral animals. Give each of them a pile of blocks. Then have them work together to pile up their "limestone" blocks to make a reef (a straight line) or an atoll (a circle).

Coral-Color Collages

Select tissue paper the colors of coral (tan, orange, yellow, purple and green) and cut it into small squares. Set out the tissue-paper squares, paintbrushes and bowls of glue. Give each of your children a piece of construction paper. Have them use the brushes to spread glue all over their papers. Then let them arrange the tissue-paper squares on the glue to create collages in coral colors.

In the Tropical Ocean

Sung to: "The Little White Duck"

In the tropical ocean

You'll find coral growing,

Building their homes

Without ever slowing.

They live together and grow so tall,

They form a reef that's just like a wall.

In the tropical ocean

You'll find coral growing,

Growing, growing tall.

Gayle Bittinger

Ocean Animals

Crab Facts

■ Crabs live on rocky, muddy or sandy seashores and are found throughout the world. They make their homes in burrows that they dig or find.

■ Crabs have a flat, broad body covered by a shell, called a carapace. Most crabs have 10 legs, four on each side of the body and two big claws, or pincers, in front.

■ Crabs use their legs to walk sideways across rocks and sand.

■ Crabs molt every year, which means they shed their old shells and grow new ones.

Crab Walk

Ask your children to sit on the floor and lean back on their hands. Have them bend their knees, keeping their feet flat on the floor. Then have them lift their bottoms off the floor and try moving sideways, the only way crabs can move. Can the children also move forward and backward?

Directions Game

Cut a crab shape out of orange construction paper, using the teaching-aid pattern on page 87 as a guide. Cover the crab shape with clear, self-stick paper. Set out four rocks of different shapes, sizes and colors. Give one of your children the crab shape and ask him or her to follow directions such as these: "Put the crab on top of the biggest rock, underneath the round rock, beside the black rock." Then give the crab to the other children, one at a time, asking each child to put the crab in a different place.

Variation: Put the crab in a specific place and ask the children to tell you where the crab is.

We're Little Orange Crabs
Sung to: "The Farmer in the Dell"

We're little orange crabs,

Who live down by the sea.

And wherever we do go,

We're quick as quick can be.

We're little orange crabs,

Who like to run and hide.

And when you see us walking by,

It's always side-to-side.

Jean Warren

Fish Facts

■ Two-thirds of all fish live in the ocean. About 21,000 different kinds of fish have been identified with various features and unique qualities. All fish have three things in common: they are vertebrates (they have backbones); they breathe through gills; and they are cold-blooded. Most fish have thin, bony scales. Some fish live together in schools.

■ Fish come in all colors. Many tropical fish are brightly colored red, yellow, blue or purple, with polka dots and stripes.

■ Fish vary in size from the 1/2-inch pygmy goby to the 60-foot whale shark.

■ Most fish have fins. Fins help fish swim and keep their balance in water. Fish move their fins with muscles.

■ Fish are able to float because of a swim, or air, bladder. A fish can inflate or deflate this bladder as needed to swim at the depth it wants.

Paper-Plate Fish

Give each of your children a paper plate with a triangular mouth-shape drawn on one side. Have the children cut out the triangles, or help them as needed. (These openings will be the mouths of the fish.) Then have them glue the triangular pieces on the opposite sides of their plates to make tails. Let the children complete their fish by coloring them as desired and drawing eyes.

Balloon Bladders

Demonstrate to your children how a fish's swim bladder helps it stay afloat. Fill a dishpan with water. Set out two identical balls of clay and a balloon. Blow up the balloon and tie it off. Carefully form one of the balls of clay around the knot in the balloon. Put both balls of clay in the water. What happens to the ball of clay with the balloon? What happens to the ball of clay without a balloon? The clay with the balloon floats because the balloon is filled with air, just as a fish can float because its swim bladder is filled with air.

I'm a Little Fishy
Sung to: "I'm a Little Teapot"

I'm a little fishy, I can swim.

Here is my tail, here is my fin.

When I want to have fun with my friends,

I wiggle my tail and dive right in.

Lynn Beaird

Jelly Fish Facts

■ Jelly fish live in the ocean, usually along the coast.

■ Jelly fish can be various colors, including pale orange, pink, blue or clear. They range in diameter from ¼ inch to 7 feet.

■ Jelly fish swim by taking water inside their bodies and then pushing it out to propel themselves.

■ Some jelly fish catch fish to eat by stinging them with their tentacles.

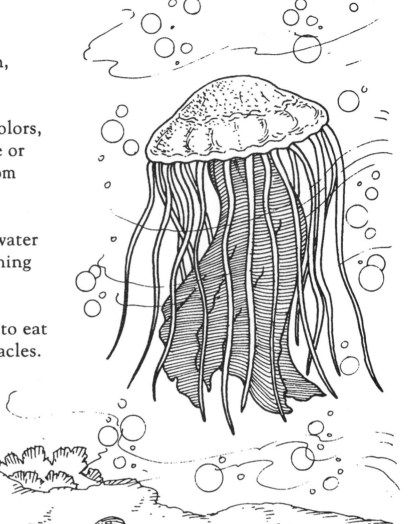

Jelly Fish Fun

Set out a large dishpan of water and some kitchen basters or squeeze bottles. Let your children pretend to be jelly fish swimming around and use the droppers to take water in and squeeze water out.

Ocean Animals

Jelly Fish Game

Attach crepe-paper streamers to a length of yarn. Select one of your children to be the Jelly Fish and tie the streamer-covered yarn around his or her waist for tentacles. Let the other children pretend to be Fish. Have the Jelly Fish chase the Fish and try to touch them with his or her "tentacles." When a Fish is caught by the Jelly Fish, it must stand still. The last Fish touched is the next Jelly Fish.

The Jelly Fish

Sung to: "My Bonnie Lies Over the Ocean"

The jelly fish lives in the ocean,

The jelly fish lives in the sea.

The jelly fish lives in the ocean,

Oh, jelly fish swim by me.

Swim, swim, swim, swim,

Oh, jelly fish swim by me, by me.

Swim, swim, swim, swim,

Oh, jelly fish swim by me.

Susan Peters

Ocean Animals

Octopus Facts

■ An octopus has a soft body and eight arms, or tentacles. On the underside of each tentacle are two rows of small, round muscles that act like suction cups.

■ An octopus has no bones nor inside shell. Its body is held together by a tough protective skin called the mantle.

■ An octopus has two eyes and sees well. It has three hearts and breathes through gills as fish do.

■ The octopus swims by drawing water into its body and expelling it to move itself backward.

■ To protect itself, the octopus can squirt out a black fluid that makes a cloud and hides the octopus from its predators.

■ Many octopuses can change their skin color to blend in with their surroundings.

Swimming Octopuses

Give each of your children a half circle cut out of white construction paper or half a paper plate for an octopus body. Let the children use black crayons to draw eyes. Then have them each glue eight pieces of white crepe paper to the bottom edges of the octopus bodies to make arms. Hang the finished octopuses from a string stetched across a window and watch them "swim" as air moves through the room.

Octopus Matching Game

Explain to your children that an octopus can change its skin color to blend in with its surroundings. Cut eight octopus shapes out of different colors of construction paper, using the teaching-aid pattern on page 85 as a guide. Draw simple seascapes on eight matching colors of construction paper. Set out the seascapes and place the octopus shapes in a pile. Have the children place each octopus on its matching background.

Eight Arms

Sung to: "Did You Ever See a Lassie?"

Once I saw an octopus, octopus, octopus,

Once I saw an octopus down deep in the sea.

Then out came her eight arms,

Her eight arms, her eight arms,

Then out came her eight arms to swim with me!

Sue Schliecker

Ocean Animals

Sea Horse Facts

■ A sea horse is a kind of fish with a head that resembles a horse's head. The sea horse moves through the water in an upright position.

■ The average sea horse is 5 inches long. Although most fish have scales, the sea horse has armor-like bony plates on its body. It has a long tail that it uses to anchor itself by coiling it around rooted plants and seaweed floating in the ocean.

■ Each female sea horse lays about 200 eggs at a time. The male keeps the eggs in a kangaroo-like pouch until they hatch.

Coiling Art

Explain to your children that sea horses use their tails to coil around objects to help them stay in place. Then give your children various colors of pipe cleaners. Let them coil the pipe cleaners around their fingers, craft sticks, chair legs, etc., to create coiled art.

Five Little Sea Horses

Cut five sea horse shapes out of felt, using the teaching-aid pattern on page 84 as a guide. Place the sea horses on a flannelboard. Recite the following poem to your children, removing a sea horse at the end of each verse.

Five little sea horses swimming near the ocean floor,
One swam away and then there were four.

Four little sea horses swimming in the deep blue sea,
One swam away and then there were three.

Three little sea horses swimming in the ocean blue,
One swam away and then there were two.

Two little sea horses swimming fast and having fun,
One swam away and then there was one.

One little sea horse swimming till the day was done,
It swam away and then there were none.

Gayle Bittinger

There Is a Horse

Sung to: "Twinkle, Twinkle, Little Star"

In the sea there is a horse,

Not like one on land, of course.

It swims all day in the blue sea

Or coils its tail around algae.

It's a sea horse, did you know?

Let's all watch the sea horse go.

Gayle Bittinger

Sea Star Facts

■ Formerly known as starfish, sea stars are not fish but are a kind of *echinoderm* (a group of animals that includes the sea urchin and sea lily).

■ Sea stars can be found in all oceans.

■ Most sea stars have five arms. Each arm has tube feet with suction disks at the ends. A sea star uses the suction disks for crawling and attaching to hard surfaces. If an arm is broken off, a sea star can regenerate (grow) a new one.

■ Sea stars come in a variety of colors such as yellow, orange, pink, red and purple.

■ A sea star's mouth is located on the underside of its body in the middle. Sea stars feed on mussels, clams and oysters.

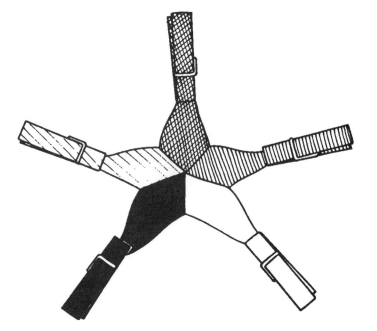

Sea Star Colors

Cut a sea star shape out of cardboard, using the teaching-aid pattern on page 87 as a guide. Color each arm of the sea star one of the following colors: yellow, orange, pink, red and purple. Collect five spring-type clothespins and color them to match. Set out the sea star and the clothespins. Let your children take turns selecting clothespins and clipping them to the appropriate arms on the sea star.

Ocean Animals

Counting Five

Since most sea stars have five arms, let your children practice counting to five in many different ways. Use the following ideas for counting or make up your own activities.

- Put away five toys.
- Pick up five pieces of litter.
- Jump up and down five times.
- Sing five songs.
- Eat five grapes for a snack.
- Make five playdough "snakes."
- Draw five circles.
- Count five pennies.
- Make five wishes.

I Am a Sea Star

Sung to: "Up on the Housetop"

I am a sea star, not a fish,

I'll tell you the difference, if you wish.

Fish have fins and swim in schools,

I have feet to wade in tide pools.

Oh, oh, oh, sea star's the name,

Ask me again and I'll tell you the same.

Fish can swim and splash all day,

Stuck to a rock I'd rather stay.

John M. Bittinger

Shark Facts

■ Sharks are considered to be meat-eating fish, although they are not really fish but a part of the family *osteochondrichthys*. They are commonly found in warm seas.

■ Sharks have no bones. Their skeletons are made of cartilage, a tough elastic substance. (The human ear gets its support from cartilage.) In fact, the name osteochondrichthys means bone-cartilage-fish.

■ A shark has several rows of teeth. When a tooth is broken or worn out, a new one grows to replace it.

■ A shark's sense of hearing is well-developed, and it can see very well in dim light. A shark also has special sensory tubes that allow it to detect electrical impulses generated by moving objects.

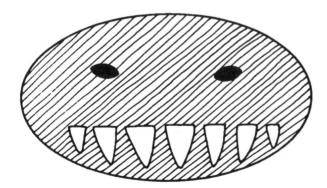

Shark Teeth Art

Give each of your children an oval cut out of gray construction paper. Set out black felt-tip markers, glue and white construction-paper tooth shapes. Let your children glue the tooth shapes on their ovals as shown in the illustration. Then have them add eyes with the felt-tip markers.

Hunting Game

Explain to your children that a shark has excellent senses of hearing and sight. Then let them practice using their hearing and sight with this game. Set a timer that ticks and hide it somewhere in your room while the children are not looking. Then have the children use their hearing and sight to find the timer before it goes off. Hide more than one timer, if desired.

The Shark

Sung to: "She'll Be Coming Round the Mountain"

Oh, the shark has lots of big sharp teeth,

Oh, the shark has lots of big sharp teeth.

Oh, the shark has lots of teeth,

Yes, the shark has lots of teeth.

Oh, the shark has lots of big sharp teeth.

Oh, the shark has cartilage for its bones,

Oh, the shark has cartilage for its bones.

Oh, the shark has cartilage,

Yes, the shark has cartilage.

Oh, the shark has cartilage for its bones.

Oh, the shark can see objects far away,

Oh, the shark can see objects far away.

Oh, the shark can see objects,

Yes, the shark can see objects.

Oh, the shark can see objects far away.

Susan A. Miller

Whale Facts

■ The largest animal that has ever lived is the blue whale. Measuring 95 feet long and weighing 150 tons, the blue whale is even larger than the biggest prehistoric dinosaurs.

■ Whales are mammals, which means they are warm-blooded and bear their young alive. They also breathe through lungs and must hold their breath when underwater. When whales return to the surface after being underwater, they "blow" their breath out blowholes.

■ Whales can be found in all oceans. Some whales live in groups called herds, schools or pods. A female whale is called a cow, a male whale a bull, and a baby whale a calf.

■ There are two kinds of whales — toothed and baleen. Toothed whales, such as sperm whales and killer whales, have teeth and eat fish and squids. Baleen whales, such as blue whales and humpback whales, have no teeth. They use their specially formed mouths to strain food, primarily plankton, out of the water.

Blue Whale Art

Hang a long piece of butcher paper on a wall. Let your children work together to paint the butcher paper blue. Allow the paint to dry, then cut the butcher paper into a blue whale shape. Display the blue whale on a wall.

Extension: Use the illustration of this activity as a guide to proportions and cut out a construction-paper elephant shape and dinosaur shape to display by your children's blue whale.

Mothers and Babies

Cut five mother whale shapes out of gray felt, using the teaching-aid pattern on page 89 as a guide. Number the mother shapes from 1 to 5. Then cut five baby whale shapes out of gray felt. Number the baby shapes with dots from 1 to 5. Place the mother shapes on a flannelboard. Let your children take turns placing the baby whale shapes on the appropriate mother whale shapes.

Salty Sea Giant

Sung to: "The Muffin Man"

Do you know a giant mammal,

Giant mammal, giant mammal?

Do you know a giant mammal

That lives in the salty sea?

Yes, it is a huge blue whale,

A huge blue whale, a huge blue whale.

Yes, it is a huge blue whale,

That lives in the salty sea.

Susan A. Miller

Ocean Animals

Ocean Preservation

Ocean Mural

Photocopy the ocean patterns on pages 82-89. Make as many copies of each pattern as desired. Cut out the patterns. Place a long piece of blue butcher paper on the floor or a table. Have your children glue the patterns on the paper any way they wish. Hang the mural on a wall or a bulletin board. If desired, cover the mural with blue cellophane to create more of an underwater effect.

Hint: Photocopy the patterns on colored paper for a more colorful mural.

Ocean Corner

Turn a corner of your room into an ocean playground. Hang green crepe-paper streamers from the ceiling for algae. Place pillow "rocks" all around. Play a tape of ocean-wave sounds. Set out books about the ocean. Hang up pictures of ocean plants and animals on the walls. Let your children read and relax in your ocean corner.

Ocean Preservation

I Live in the Ocean

Discuss with your children animals that live in the ocean and animals that do not. Then say the name of an animal. If the animal lives in the ocean, have the children make wave motions with their hands. If the animal does not live in the ocean, have your children keep their hands in their laps.

Ocean Rhyme

Read the following rhyme to your children. Encourage them to hold up the appropriate number of fingers with each verse.

Ten little crabs who lived in the sea
Jumped in the boat with Skipper and me.

Nine little fish who lived in the sea
Jumped in the boat with Skipper and me.

Eight little sea horses who lived in the sea
Jumped in the boat with Skipper and me.

Seven little oysters who lived in the sea
Jumped in the boat with Skipper and me.

Six little jelly fish who lived in the sea
Jumped in the boat with Skipper and me.

Five little sea stars who lived in the sea
Jumped in the boat with Skipper and me.

Four little octopuses who lived in the sea
Jumped in the boat with Skipper and me.

Three little sharks who lived in the sea
Jumped in the boat with Skipper and me.

Two little seals who lived in the sea
Jumped in the boat with Skipper and me.

One little whale who lived in the sea
Jumped in the boat with Skipper and me.

Jean Warren

Ocean Preservation

Web of Life

Photocopy the ocean patterns on pages 82-89. Cut out the patterns and give each of your children one to tape to his or her shirt. Have the children pretend to be the plants and animals shown on their shirts. Ask the children to stand in a circle. Give a large ball of yarn to one child. Have that child hold the yarn and toss the ball to another child. Repeat until each child is holding a section of the yarn and the web is complete. Explain to your children that the web represents the web of life in the ocean. Each plant or animal is connected to all the others in some way. Then, one at a time, have your children pretend their plants or animals have disappeared from the ocean and have them let go of the yarn. What happens to the web after one child lets go? After three children let go? After five? The web starts falling apart. When each part of the ocean is taken care of, the web of life can stay together, just as the yarn web did when all the children were holding it.

Let's Take Care of Every One
Sung to: "Twinkle, Twinkle, Little Star"

Seaweed, sea stars, giant whales,

Coral, crabs and fish with tails.

They live in the ocean blue,

And make a web of life, it's true.

Let's take care of every one,

For our job is never done.

Gayle Bittinger

Ocean Preservation

What's in the Water?

Fill three bowls with water. Add vegetable oil to one bowl and liquid soap to another. Leave one bowl as is. Set out the bowls. Let your children feel the water in the bowls. Ask them to describe what they feel. What do they think is in each bowl? Which bowl would fish like to swim in? Explain to them that oil and soap are two kinds of things that get into the ocean and pollute it.

Oil Spill

Place a pie pan or a cake pan on a table for each of your children. Fill the pans halfway with water. Set out spoons, cotton balls, fabric scraps, aluminum foil, plastic netting and craft sticks on the table. Explain to your children that one of the ways the ocean gets polluted is when oil is spilled or dumped into it. Have each child sit by a pan and pretend that it is the ocean. Ask the children to guess what will happen when you pour oil on their water. Then pour a 1/8-inch layer of vegetable oil on top of the water in each pan. Have the children use the objects on the table, or any others they can think of, to try removing the oil from the water. What is happening to the oil and water? Is it easy or hard to remove the oil? If there were animals living in the water, what would be happening to them?

Water Garbage

Fill a cardboard box with various kinds of garbage such as a plastic bag, a plastic bottle, a newspaper, an aluminum can and a glass jar. Explain to your children that when people litter some of their garbage can end up in the ocean. This garbage makes the ocean dirty, and it can also hurt the fish and other animals that live there. Then set out the box you prepared. Tell the children that this box is filled with some of the kinds of garbage that ends up in our water. Ask one of the children to take a piece of garbage out of the box and identify it. Then sing the song at right, inserting the name of the piece of garbage in the blanks. Repeat until each child has had a turn taking out a piece of garbage. After all the children have had turns, let them throw their garbage in a trash can or an appropriate recycling bin.

Sung to: "The Bear Went Over the Mountain"

There's something polluting our water,

There's something polluting our water,

There's something polluting our water,

I'll tell you what it is.

It is a _____,

It is a _____,

It is a _____,

Yucky, yucky, poo.

(Hold nose.)

Jean Warren

Look and Gently Touch

Explain to your children that whenever they explore the beach and ocean, they must remember the rule: "Leave it where you find it." Many animals and plants make their homes on the ocean beaches, and they do not want to be disturbed or moved around. Tell your children they may look at and gently touch the plants and animals they see, but they must leave them where they are. Take your children on a walk outside to practice this rule.

I Will Care For

Sung to: "Oh, My Darling Clementine"

I will care for,

I will care for,

I will care for the ocean.

I will keep the waters clean,

I will care for the ocean.

Additional verses: I will throw my trash in cans; I will leave things where I found them.

Gayle Bittinger

Ocean Preservation

Ocean Patterns

Seaweed

Scuba Diver

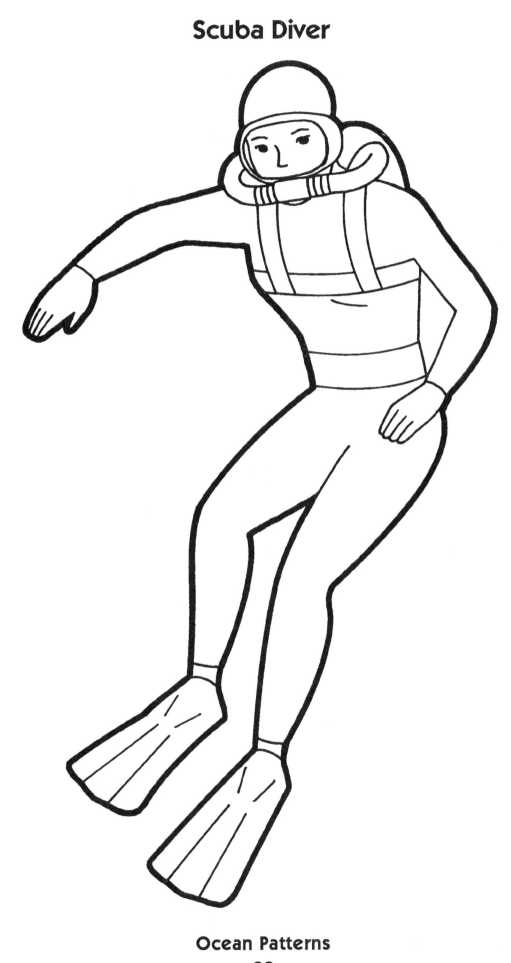

Ocean Patterns

Coral

Sea Horse

Ocean Patterns

Octopus

Fish

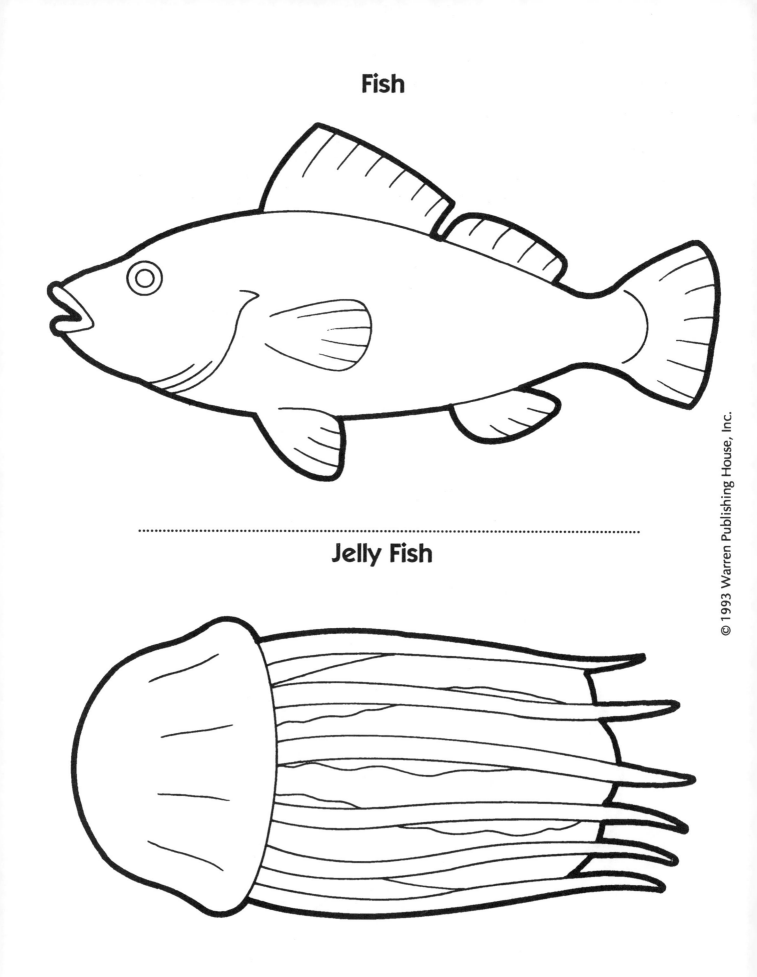

Jelly Fish

Crab

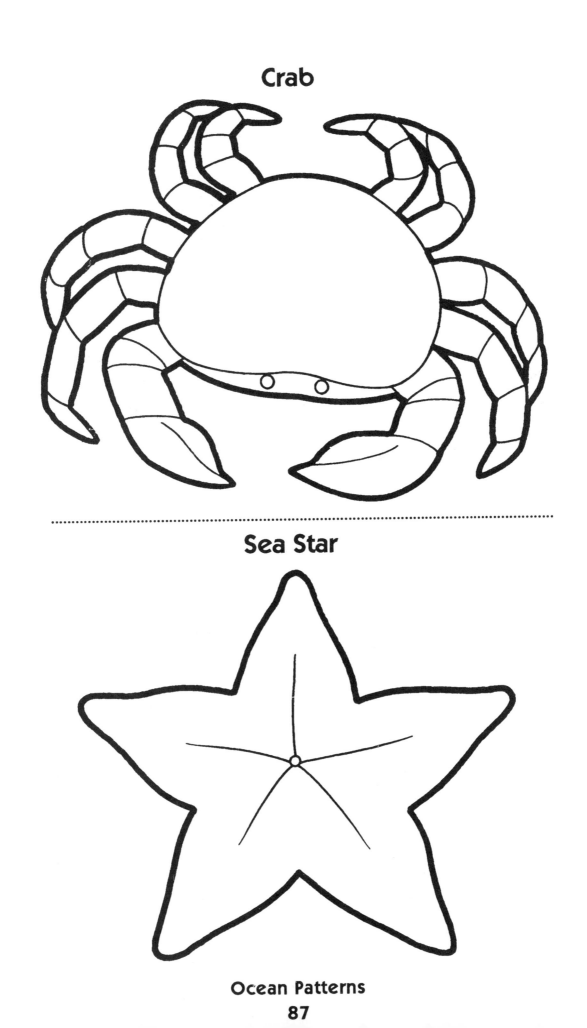

Sea Star

Shark

Ocean Patterns

Whale

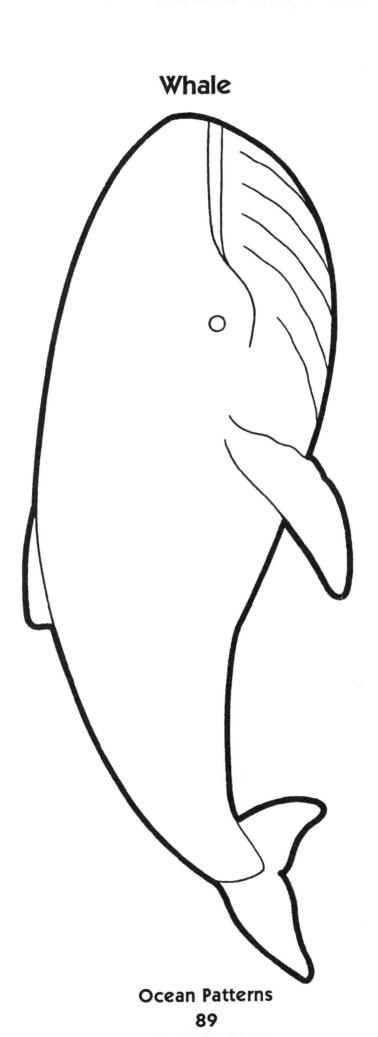

Ocean Patterns

CHILDREN'S BOOKS ABOUT WATER AND THE OCEAN

FICTION

Baby Beluga, Raffi, (Crown, 1992).

Dear Mr. Blueberry, Simon James, (Macmillan, 1991).

Fish Eyes, Lois Ehlert,
    (Harcourt Brace Jovanovich, 1992).

Harry by the Sea, Gene Zion, (Harper & Row, 1976).

One World, Michael Foreman, (Little Brown, 1991).

Swimmy, Leo Lionni, (Knopf, 1987).

NON-FICTION

Down in the Sea: the Jellyfish, Patricia Kite,
    (Albert Whitman, 1992).

Down in the Sea: the Octopus, Patricia Kite,
    (Albert Whitman, 1992).

A House for Hermit Crab, Eric Carle,
    (Picture Book Studio, 1991).

How to Hide an Octopus, Ruth Heller,
    (Putnam, 1986).

Is This a House for Hermit Crab?, Megan McDonald,
    (Orchard, 1990).

Ocean, Ron Hirschi, (Bantam, 1991).

Sharks, Gail Gibbons, (Holiday House, 1992).

Under the Sea from A to Z, Anne Doubilet,
    (Crown, 1991).

Underwater Alphabet Book, Jerry Pallotta,
    (Charlesbridge, 1991).

Whales, Gail Gibbons, (Holiday House, 1991).

When the Tide Is Low, Shiela Cole, (Morrow, 1985).

1001 SERIES

These super reference books are filled with just the right solution, prop, or poem to get your projects going. Creative, inexpensive ideas await you!

1001 Teaching Props

The ultimate how-to prop book to plan projects and equip discovery centers. Comprehensive materials index lets you create projects with recyclable materials. 248 pp.
WPH 1501 • $19.95

1001 Teaching Tips

Shortcuts to success for busy teachers on limited budgets. Curriculum, room, and special times tips—even a subject index. 208 pp.
WPH 1502 • $17.95

1001 Rhymes & Fingerplays

A complete language resource for parents and teachers! Rhymes for all occasions, plus poems about self-esteem, families, special needs, and more. 312 pp.
WPH 1503 • $23.95

For Two's and Three's

BUSY BEES

Seasonal, hands-on projects and activities that are just right for busy little ones.

Busy Bees—FALL

For fall fun and learning, these attention-getting activities include songs, rhymes, snacks, movements, art, and science projects. 136 pp.
WPH 2405 • $14.95

Busy Bees—WINTER

Enchant toddlers through winter with a wealth of seasonal ideas, from movement to art. 136 pp.
WPH 2406 • $14.95

Busy Bees—SPRING

More than 60 age-appropriate activities enhance learning for busy minds and bodies. 136 pp.
WPH 2407 • $14.95

Busy Bees—SUMMER

Encourage toddlers to build, develop, and explore with their senses and turn summer fun into learning. 136 pp.
WPH 2408 • $14.95

THEME-A-SAURUS

Capture special teaching moments with instant theme ideas that cover around-the-curriculum activities.

Theme-A-Saurus

56 teaching themes—from Apples to Zebras—plus 600 fun and educational activity ideas. 280 pp.
WPH 1001 • $21.95

Theme-A-Saurus II

Sixty more teaching units—from Ants to Zippers—for hands-on learning experiences. 280 pp.
WPH 1002 • $21.95

Toddler Theme-A-Saurus

Sixty teaching themes combine safe, appropriate materials with creative activity ideas. 280 pp.
WPH 1003 • $21.95

Alphabet Theme-A-Saurus

From A to Z—26 giant letter recognition units filled with hands-on activities introduce young children to the *ABC's*. 280 pp.
WPH 1004 • $21.95

Nursery Rhyme Theme-A-Saurus

Capture the interest children have for nursery rhymes and extend it into learning. 160 pp.
WPH 1005 • $14.95

Storytime Theme-A-Saurus

Character patterns, game ideas, and songs accompany 12 storytime favorites adapted for young children. 160 pp.
WPH 1006 • $14.95

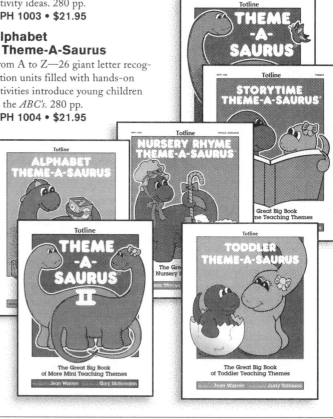

Perfect for the beginning teacher!

THE BEST OF TOTLINE SERIES

The best ideas from more than a decade of Totline newsletters! This around-the-curriculum resource guide is for use with ages 3 to 6.

The Best of Totline Newsletter

A year of art, music, movement, science, math, and snacks in one giant resource! 400 pp.
WPH 2601 • $27.95

1•2•3 SERIES

It's as easy as 1-2-3 to round out your curriculum with this series. The simple, hands-on activities reflect Totline's commitment to providing open-ended, age-appropriate, cooperative, and no-lose experiences for working with preschool children.

1•2•3 Art
Art activities to emphasize the creative process. All 238 activities use inexpensive, readily available materials. 160 pp.
WPH 0401 • $14.95

1•2•3 Games
Foster creativity and decision-making with 70 no-lose games for a variety of young ages. 80 pp.
WPH 0402 • $8.95

1•2•3 Colors
Hundreds of activities for Color Days, including art, learning games, language, science, movement, music, and snacks. 160 pp.
WPH 0403 • $14.95

1•2•3 Puppets
More than 50 simple puppets to make to delight children. 80 pp.
WPH 0404 • $8.95

1•2•3 Reading & Writing
50 meaningful and nonthreatening activities to develop pre-reading and pre-writing skills. 160 pp.
WPH 0407 • $14.95

1•2•3 Rhymes, Stories & Songs
Open-ended rhymes, stories, and songs for young children. 80 pp.
WPH 0408 • $8.95

1•2•3 Math
Hands-on activities, such as counting, sequencing, and sorting, help develop pre-math skills. 160 pp.
WPH 0409 • $14.95

1•2•3 Science
Develop science skills—observing, estimating, predicting—using ordinary household objects. 160 pp.
WPH 0410 • $14.95

1•2•3 Shapes
Hundreds of activities for exploring the concept of shapes—circles, squares, triangles, rectangles, ovals, diamonds, hearts, and stars. 160 pp.
WPH 0411 • $14.95

BEAR HUGS® SERIES

This unique series focuses on positive behavior in young children and how to encourage it. Bear Hugs books can put the fun back into teaching while getting desired results. Each 24 pp.

The first set of Bear Hugs books emphasizes positive ways to deal with potential problem times. Each book offers great ideas for handling specific group situations.

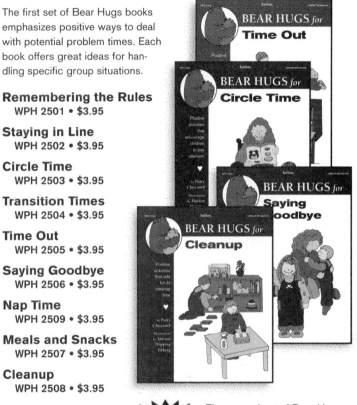

Remembering the Rules
WPH 2501 • $3.95

Staying in Line
WPH 2502 • $3.95

Circle Time
WPH 2503 • $3.95

Transition Times
WPH 2504 • $3.95

Time Out
WPH 2505 • $3.95

Saying Goodbye
WPH 2506 • $3.95

Nap Time
WPH 2509 • $3.95

Meals and Snacks
WPH 2507 • $3.95

Cleanup
WPH 2508 • $3.95

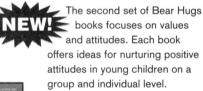

NEW!

The second set of Bear Hugs books focuses on values and attitudes. Each book offers ideas for nurturing positive attitudes in young children on a group and individual level.

Saving the Earth
WPH 2510 • $3.95

Getting Along
WPH 2511 • $3.95

Fostering Self-Esteem
WPH 2512 • $3.95

Being Afraid
WPH 2513 • $3.95

Being Responsible
WPH 2514 • $3.95

Being Healthy
WPH 2515 • $3.95

Welcoming Children
WPH 2516 • $3.95

Accepting Change
WPH 2517 • $3.95

Respecting Others
WPH 2518 • $3.95

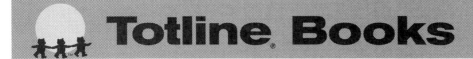

Repetition & Rhyme
PIGGYBACK® SONGS SERIES

New songs sung to the tunes of childhood favorites. No music to read! Easy for both adults and children to learn. Chorded for guitar or autoharp.

Piggyback Songs
A seasonal collection of more than 100 original, easy-to-sing songs for children! 64 pp.
WPH 0201 • $7.95

More Piggyback Songs
More seasonal songs fill this delightful 180-song collection. 96 pp.
WPH 0202 • $8.95

Piggyback Songs for Infants & Toddlers
This special collection of more than 170 songs is just right for infants and toddlers. Also appropriate for children ages 3 to 5. 80 pp.
WPH 0203 • $8.95

Holiday Piggyback Songs
More than 250 original songs for young children to sing for 15 major holidays and celebrations. 96 pp.
WPH 0206 • $8.95

Animal Piggyback Songs
More than 200 songs about farm, zoo, and sea animals. 96 pp.
WPH 0207 • $8.95

Piggyback Songs for School
Delightful songs to use throughout the school day: songs for getting acquainted, transition, storytime, movement, and cleanup. Use music to help teach basic concepts. 96 pp.
WPH 0208 • $8.95

Piggyback Songs to Sign
Teach your children four seasonal signing phrases for each month of the year, plus three to four songs that use each signing phrase. 96 pp.
WPH 0209 • $8.95

Spanish Piggyback Songs
Ideal for introducing simple Spanish or English phrases and words. Spanish translations and pronunciation guides included for all songs. 64 pp.
WPH 0210 • $7.95

NEW! More Piggyback Songs for School
Many new songs for the school day. Reinforce learning by combining concepts with music. Or sing the songs just for fun! 80 pp.
WPH 0211 • $8.95

Piggyback® Songs are now available on Cassette, LP, and CD!

NEW!

Your favorite singable songs from Totline's original *Piggyback Songs* book are now available on special recordings from Kimbo Educational. Filled with captivating tunes, Piggyback Songs (on cassette, LP, or compact disc) will have your children singing and dancing—and learning too. Learning comes alive for children when they can hear Piggyback Songs set to music. The recordings include songs about the four seasons, plus songs about self-awareness and school. Encourage your children to:

♪ Sing along with the voices on the recordings.

♪ Dramatize the actions in the songs.

♪ Make up their own lyrics to the tunes.

If you are a parent, preschool teacher, librarian, or caregiver—you will love the way your children respond to these simple, yet meaningful songs.

Piggyback Songs on Cassette Tape
39 songs
KE01 • $10.95

Piggyback Songs on LP
39 songs
KE21 • $11.95

Piggyback Songs on Compact Disc
39 songs
KE41 • $14.95

Teacher Resources

EXPLORING SERIES

Selected environments become very real places through hands-on activities that emphasize all the curriculum areas. Set up child-directed learning units!

Exploring Sand and the Desert
WPH 1801 • $8.95

Exploring Water and the Ocean
WPH 1802 • $8.95

Exploring Wood and the Forest
WPH 1803 • $8.95

LEARNING & CARING ABOUT

Developmentally appropriate activities to help children explore, understand, and appreciate the world around them—plus reproducible parent flyers.

Environmental Awareness

Our World
WPH 1201 • $8.95

Self-Awareness

Our Selves
WPH 1202 • $8.95

Social Awareness

Our Town
WPH 1203 • $8.95

CELEBRATIONS

Expand on your children's love for celebrations with these ideas for special learning fun.

Multicultural Units • 160 pp.
Small World Celebrations
WPH 0701 • $14.95

Nontraditional Units • 128 pp.
Special Day Celebrations
WPH 0702 • $14.95

Traditional Units • 228 pp.
Great Big Holiday Celebrations
WPH 0704 • $17.95

PLAY & LEARN

This creative series explores the versatile play-and-learn opportunities of familiar objects. Each 64-page book offers more than 100 fun and educational ideas for turning simple materials into learning games, art activities, storytime fun, and more! Perfect for working with young children ages 3 to 5.

NEW! **Play & Learn with Paper Shapes and Borders**
WPH 2304 • $7.95

NEW! **Play & Learn with Stickers**
WPH 2305 • $7.95

Play & Learn with Magnets
WPH 2301 • $7.95

Play & Learn with Rubber Stamps
WPH 2302 • $7.95

Play & Learn with Photos
WPH 2303 • $7.95

Food & Nutrition

SNACKS SERIES

Nutritious snacks for home or school and additional learning opportunities.

Super Snacks
Seasonal recipes with no sugar, honey, or artificial sweeteners! 48 pp.
WPH 1601 • $6.95

Healthy Snacks
New recipes for healthy snacks low in fat, sugar, and sodium. 48 pp.
WPH 1602 • $6.95

Teaching Snacks
Use snacktime to promote basic skills and concepts. 48 pp.
WPH 1603 • $6.95

Multicultural Snacks
Recipes from 38 countries let children get a taste of many cultures. Each chapter features one food and different ways to prepare it. 48 pp.
WPH 1604 • $6.95

Instant, hands-on activity ideas for working with young children

Totline® Newsletter

This newsletter offers creative hands-on activities that are designed to be challenging for children ages 2 to 6, yet easy for teachers and parents to do. Minimal preparation time is needed to make maximum use of common, inexpensive materials. Each bimonthly issue includes seasonal fun plus • learning games • open-ended art • music and movement • language activities • science fun • reproducible teaching aids • reproducible parent-flyer pages and • toddler activities. *Totline Newsletter* is perfect for use with an antibias curriculum or to emphasize multicultural values in a home environment.

Reproducible!

Super Snack News

This newsletter is designed to be reproduced!

With each subscription you are permitted to make up to 200 copies per issue! They make great handouts for parents. Inside this monthly, four-page newsletter are healthy recipes and nutrition tips, plus related songs and activities for young children. Also provided are category guidelines for the Child and Adult Care Food Program (CACFP). Sharing *Super Snack News* is a wonderful way to help promote parent involvement in quality childcare.